THE TOTALLY AWESOME DAD JOKE BOOK

New and Revised Edition

Zack Halliday

CONTENTS

Welcome to this new edition of The Totally Awesome Dad Joke Book. Full of great Dad Jokes. **Lots of new jokes for 2022.**

This book is for having fun, reading or sending as a present. **Over 550 fun, family-rated jokes you can enjoy.**

We wrote the book to give as a great gift. Use the paperback as a stocking stuffer or send the Kindle version (to be read on any device, phone, tablet, laptop or Kindle,) as an online present and, if needed, as a last minute gift!

Give it to your Dad, husband or to any father, **(he can keep the Kindle version on his phone, ready at any time to tell a great joke.)**

We all love to tell jokes to our kids or to other members of the family. With this book laughs are guaranteed!

We hope you enjoy. If you do, please tell others about our book, and please, leave us positive feedback with Amazon and perhaps a high star rating…. It is really important to us and we would greatly appreciated it.

Thank you. Zack Halliday

DAD, FRONT AND CENTER!

· Dad was upset, somebody had glued his cards together. **He didn't know how to deal with it!**

· What does Dad call a blind dinosaur? **A Doyouthinkitsaurus!**

· And what does he call a blind dinosaur's dog? **A Doyouthinkitsaurus Rex.**

· Dad says, 'Kids, you can pick your friends and you can pick your nose. **But you can't**

pick your friend's nose!'

• Dad said to Mom, 'how come nobody ever listens to me?' **She said, 'sorry, what was that?'**

• Dad says he's so good at sleeping **he can do it with his eyes closed!**

• I told Dad a chemical joke. **But I didn't get a reaction!**

• When he's bored, Dad rings Best Western Hotels and when they reply with 'Best Western.' **He answers with, 'True Grit with John Wayne.' Then roars with laughter.**

- Mom says Dad is afraid of elevators. **But he's taking steps to deal with it!**

- Dad said, looking up, 'I really like this ceiling. **It's not the best ceiling in the world but it's right up there!'**

- Dad says his favorite pen can write underwater. **It can write other words as well but underwater is one of his favorites!**

- Dad started investing in stocks… first was chicken, then beef, and then vegetables. **He says it's risky but one day it will pay off and he'll be a bouillonaire!**

- Can Mom tell a Dad Joke? **Or would that be a faux pa!**

- The reason Dad talks to himself, as he says, **sometimes he needs an expert opinion!**

- What's Dad's new seafood diet? **He sees food and he eats it!**

- Dad says the patron saint of humor is **St. Francis of Hee Hee!**

- Dad says middle age is when the glass is still half full. **Mom says that's true but soon his** teeth will be floating in it!

- Dad says he's only pushing forty. **Mom says he's clinging on to it for dear life.**

- Dad says he's still broad minded and narrow waisted. **Mom says soon those will be changing places.**

- Why did Dad throw the butter out the window? **He wanted to see a butterfly!**

- Dad is reading a book about anti-gravity. **He says it's impossible to put down!**

· A family leaves Disney after a long day there. As they leave the son waves out the window and says, "goodbye Mickey." The daughter waves and says, "goodbye Minnie." **Dad waves and says, "goodbye money!"**

· Dad says the pen is mightier than the sword. **Mom says she agrees if the sword is tiny and the pen is really sharp!**

· Mom asked Dad if he was indecisive. **He said, 'Well, yes and no!'**

· My Dad told me a joke about boxing. **I didn't get it, I guess**

I missed the punchline!

- Dad asked mom, 'do you find me dark and handsome?' **She said, 'In the dark I find you handsome!'**

- Dad once tried to eat a clock. **He found it very time consuming!**

- When does a joke become a 'dad joke?' **When it becomes apparent!**

- Dad, did you get a haircut? **'No, I got all of them cut!'**

- Mom says Dad was born

upside down, **his nose runs and his feet smell!**

- Why do dads take an extra pair of socks when they go golfing? **In case they get a hole-in-one**!

- Dad said, 'It was a lovely wedding, **even the cake was in tiers!**

- Dad says dogs can't operate MRI machines. **But catscan!**

- Dad gave away all his dead batteries today. **Free of charge!**

• Dad hosts a book reading club at a prison, but he's not sure he likes it. **Says it has its prose and cons though!**

• Mom asked Dad how he liked his new beard? **He's not sure but it's starting to grow on him!**

• Dad had a word with mom the other day. **Opened with, 'long time listener, first time talker!'**

• The youngest set fire to the house. **Dad, with his arm around Mom and with tears in his eyes said, 'That's arson!'**

• Dad says that women have
the last word in an argument -
**anything a man says after that is
the start of a new argument!**

• Dad said that for their anniversary
Mom let him do something
he'd always dreamed of - **she
let him win an argument!**

• Mom insists she will meet
Dad halfway in an argument
- **when he admits he's wrong
then she'll admit she's right!**

• The waiter asked Dad, 'how
do you want your steak?' 'Like

how often I win an argument with my wife,' replied Dad. **The waiter replied, 'rare it is, sir!'**

• At the restaurant the waiter said, 'do you want a box for your leftovers?' **And Dad said, 'no, but I'll wrestle you for them!'**

• Dad told Mom she should embrace her mistakes. **So she gave him a big hug!**

• So my mom held it up and said, 'look at this, it still fits me after 25 years.' **'Yes,' Dad said, 'it's a good scarf, that.'**

- My dad said, 'starting tomorrow whatever life throws at me, **I'm ducking so it hits someone else.'**

- I don't always tell Dad jokes. **But when I do he usually laughs!**

- My dad told my Mom, 'you'll never find another me.' **Not sure if that's a good thing or bad but it's the truth!**

- My mom asked my dad why he spoke so softly in the house. He said he was afraid Mark Zuckerberg was listening. She laughed, my dad laughed... **then Alexa and Siri also laughed!**

• Dad stayed up all night wondering where the sun went. **Then it dawned on him!**

• Dad says, time flies like an arrow. **But fruit flies like a banana!**

• Dad says without geometry **life is pointless!**

• Dad was hit on the head with a can of Sprite. **He's okay, it was a soft drink!**

• Son: 'What exactly is an acorn?' **Dad: 'Well, in a nutshell, it's an oak tree!'**

- Dad said, for a Christmas present he is going to buy mom a fridge. **Says, 'when she opens it I bet her face lights up!'**

- Mom said she gets mad when somebody steals her utensils. **Dad said, that's a whisk he's willing to take!**

- Mom asked dad to pick up 6 cans of Sprite from the supermarket. **But when he got home he realized he'd picked 7 Up!**

- Dad said he wished Covid had

started in Las Vegas. **Because what happens in Vegas stays in Vegas!**

- Dad, can you put my shoes on? **No, I don't think they will fit me.**

- Mom asked dad the difference between ignorance and apathy. **He said he didn't know and he didn't care!**

DAD CHRISTMAS JOKES

- How much does it cost Santa to park his sleigh? **Nothing, it's on the house!**

- What do Santa's little helpers learn at school? **The elf-abet!**

- What do they sing at a snowman's birthday party? **Freeze a jolly good fellow!**

- What do angry mice send each other at Christmas? **Cross-mouse cards!**

- If runners get athlete's foot, what do elves get? **Mistle-toes.**

- What do English teachers call Santa's elves? **Subordinate Clauses.**

- What's the coldest Christmas food? **Pigs in blankets!**

- What do you get if you cross Santa with a duck? **A Christmas Quacker!**

- Who is a Christmas tree's favorite singer? **Spruce Springsteen.**

• What do icemen have for breakfast? **Snowflakes!**

• But what do they eat for lunch? **Icebergers!**

• What is Santa's favorite State to deliver presents? **Idaho-ho-ho!**

• How is the alphabet different at Christmas? **It has Noel in it.**

• How did Darth Vadar know what Luke got him for Christmas? **He felt his present!**

- Who is the favorite singer at Santa's Workshop? **Elfish Presley.**

- What do you call a poor Santa Claus? **St. Nickel-less!**

- Why don't you ever see Santa in hospital? **Because he has private elf-care!**

- What song do the Monkeys sing at Christmas? **Jungle Bells.**

- How do they teach reading at the North Pole Elementary School? **They learn the elf-abet.**

- Who is Rudolph's favorite singer? **Beyon-sleigh!**

- Who delivers presents to baby sharks at Christmas? **Santa-Jaws!**

- What kind of motorbike does Santa ride? **A Holly Davidson!**

- What did Adam say the day before Christmas? **It's Christmas, Eve!**

- What do reindeer say before telling a joke? **This one will sleigh you!**

- What do elves cook with in the kitchen? **Utinsels!**

- What game do reindeer play at sleepovers? **Truth or deer!**

- What is the name of Santa's dog? **Santa Paws!**

- What's red and white and falls down chimneys? **Santa Klutz!**

- What did one Christmas tree say to the other? **Lighten up!**

- Knock, knock! Who's there? Mary. Mary who? **Mary Christmas!**

- Knock, knock! Who's there? Honda. Honda who? **Honda first day of Christmas my true love said to me...**

- Knock, knock! Who's there? Dexter. Dexter who? **Dexter halls with boughs of holly...**

DAD SCHOOL JOKES

- What did one pencil say to the other on first day at school? **Looking sharp!**

- I flunked my chemistry test. **I didn't have the concentration!**

- What type of math is a forestry student good at? **Logarithms!**

- 6 was scared of 7 because 7,8,9. **4 witnessed everything but was 2 squared to tell anyone!**

- I wanted to make a joke about sodium. **But then I was Na, people wouldn't get it!**

- Where do math teachers go on vacation? **Times Square!**

- Where do young trees go to learn? **Elementree school!**

- Did you hear about the kidnapping at school. **It's okay, the teacher woke her up!**

- What contest do skunks win at school? **The smelling bee!**

- Dear Math, **grow up and solve your own problems!**

- Why was the broom late for class? **It over-swept!**

- Did you know that **five out of four students are poor at fractions!**

- Did you know seven has 'even' in it? **That's odd!**

- The difference between a numerator and a denominator is a short line. **Only a fraction of people will understand this!**

- Did you hear of the mathematician who's afraid of negative numbers? **He'll stop at nothing to avoid them!**

- Why did the math book look so sad? **Because of all the problems!**

- Did you hear about Pennywise's immature younger brother? **He's pound foolish!**

- A teacher approaches the desk of a student during an exam. 'I hope I didn't just see you looking at your neighbors answers?' The student replies, **'I hope you didn't see it either!'**

- What did you learn in school today? **Not enough, I have to go back tomorrow!**

- What object is the king of the classroom? **The ruler!**

- What did the pencil sharpener say to the pencil? **Stop going round in circles and get to the point!**

- How does the science teacher freshen her breath? **With experi-mints!**

- Why did the teacher wear

dark glasses to school? **Because her students were so bright!**

- What dinosaur has the best vocabulary? **The thesaurus!**

- What did the paper say to the pencil? **Write on!**

- Why do magicians always do so well at school? **Because they can handle trick questions!**

- Where do surfers go to school? **Boarding school!**

• What does a book do in winter? **Puts on a jacket!**

• What flies around the kindergarten room at night? **The alpha-Bat!**

• What do you get if you cross a teacher with a tiger? **I don't know but you had better behave!**

• What's the worst thing that can happen to a geography teacher? **Getting lost!**

• Where do birds go to

learn? **High school!**

• Why are school cafeteria workers cruel? **Because they batter fish, beat eggs and whip cream!**

• What did the science teacher say to the hydrogen atom that claimed it had lost an electron? **'Are you positive?'**

• What do you get when you cross one principal with another? **I wouldn't do it, principals don't like to be crossed!**

• What do you get when you

cross a teacher and a vampire? **Lots of blood tests!**

- What does a thesaurus eat for breakfast? **A synonym roll!**

- What did the cross-eyed teacher say to the principal? '**I can't control my pupils!**'

- What did the student say to the math worksheet? '**I'm not a therapist, solve your own problems!**'

DAD'S JOKES ABOUT RELATIONSHIPS

• What did Mom say when she won an award for her baking? **It was a piece of cake!**

• Mom says to be happy with a man you must love him a little and understand him a lot. **Dad says to be happy with a woman you must love her a lot and try not to understand her at all!**

• Mom says that Dad's idea of doing housework is **lifting his feet while she vacuums.**

- Dad says there are two rules for dealing with women. **Unfortunately nobody knows what they are!**

- Dad also says there are two rules for arguing with women. **Again, unfortunately, neither of them works!**

- Dad says, never tell a woman you're unworthy of her love. **She knows!**

- Dad says if you think women are the weaker sex **try pulling the blankets back to your side of the bed!**

- Dad's advice, 'Ladies, if he doesn't appreciate your fruit puns... **you need to let that mango!'**

- Dad says when Mom finds out he's replaced the bed with a trampoline **she is going to hit the roof!**

- Never go out with a tennis player. **Love means nothing to them!**

- I took my young daughter to the office on 'Bring Your Child to Work Day.' She started crying. With my colleagues gathered round, she sobbed, **'Daddy, where are all the clowns you said you worked with?'**

• My girlfriend said, 'You act like a detective too much. I want to split up.' 'Good idea,' I replied. **'We can cover more ground that way!'**

• My wife said I never buy her flowers - **I didn't even know she sold flowers!**

• Mom says she and Dad are going to have matching Halloween costumes. **She's going as a deadbolt and he's a little dorky!**

• What did the mommy bullet say to the daddy bullet? **We're going to have a BB!**

- Few women admit their age. **Few men act it!**

- Nobody will ever win the battle of the sexes, **there's too much fraternizing with the enemy!**

- Do you know the last thing my granddad said to me before he kicked the bucket? He said, **'Kid, watch how far I can kick this bucket!'**

- I used to run a dating service for chickens. **But I was struggling to makes hens meet!**

• A dad confronts his young son, 'I heard you skipped school today to go to the beach with your friends.' 'That's not true,' replies the boy. **'And I've got the movie stub to prove it!'**

• I carry a picture of my wife and kids in my wallet. **It reminds me why there's no money in it!**

• I told my girlfriend she drew her eyebrows too high. **She looked surprised!**

• My wife told me to stop acting like a flamingo. **So I put my foot down!**

• I don't believe in astrology, said Mom. **I'm a Sagittarius and we're known for being skeptical!**

• My wife just accused me of having zero empathy. **I just don't understand why she feels that way!**

• My wife says I should do lunges to stay in shape. **That would be a big step forward!**

• Dad says middle age is when your **age starts showing around your middle!**

• Mom says his get up and go

has **gotten up and gone!**

- Middle age is when women stop worrying about being pregnant, and **men start worrying they look like they are!**

- Mom says dad is so old **they've cancelled his blood type!**

- Mom says when dad was young **everything was in black and white!**

- Mom says dad's not that old, **but when he was young he did play with dinosaurs!**

- A husband and wife were arguing. "We're just not compatible," said the wife. **"I'm an Aries and you're a buffoon!"**

- My grandad checks the obituaries each morning as soon as he gets up. **He can't have breakfast till he makes sure his name isn't there!**

- My grandpa saw the Titanic sinking. He even warned everyone that it would sink but nobody listened. **Later he was kicked out of the moviehouse!**

- My neighbor has erected a nine foot

fence. **I'm so upset, I can't get over it!**

• The wife's always putting me down in front of others. **I guess I'm a bit heavy for piggy back rides.**

DAD'S COMPUTER JOKES

- Why is the Apple store so hot? **Because they won't install Windows!**

- To whoever stole my copy of Microsoft Office, I will find you. **You have my Word!**

- How did the hacker escape the police? **He just ransomware!**

- The ancestry website tried to fool me into thinking I'm Swedish, but I refuse to believe it. **I wasn't Bjorn yesterday!**

- What do you get when you cross a computer and a life guard? **A screensaver!**

- And what do you get when you cross a computer with an elephant? **Lots of memory!**

- What's a robot's favorite snack? **Computer chips!**

- Why are spiders really good at the internet? **They know all the best websites!**

- What does a baby computer

call his father? **Data!**

- If you see a crime at an Apple store, **does that make you an iWitness?**

- Dad says Forrest Gump's computer password is **1forrest1**

- What's an astronaut's favorite part of a computer? **The space bar!**

- What do computers do on a beach vacation? **They surf the net!**

- How is a computer like a grandparent? **The first thing that**

goes for both is the memory!

• Dad hates it when his computer goes down and the resident computer expert isn't available - **because he's six years old and it's past his bedtime!**

• What's the biggest fib in the universe? **'I have read and agree to the Terms and Conditions.'**

• How many programmers does it take to change a lightbulb? **None, it's a hardware problem!**

• I changed my password to 'incorrect'. So whenever I forget it the computer will say, '**your password is incorrect**'.

• A computer once beat me
at chess, **but it was no match
for me at kick boxing!**

• It's okay computer, **Dad also goes to
sleep after 20 minutes of inactivity!**

• Dad entered what he'd eaten today
into his fitness app **and it sent
an ambulance to the house!**

• The wifi went down during family
dinner tonight. **A kid started talking
and I didn't know who it was!**

- I would like to thank everybody that stuck by my side **for those five long minutes my house didn't have internet tonight!**

- What did the computer do at lunchtime? **It had a byte!**

- Why did the computer keep sneezing? **It had a virus!**

- Why did the computer squeak? **Because somebody stepped on its mouse!**

- Where do all the cool mice

live? **In their mousepads!**

• Why are people afraid of computers? **They byte!**

• How did the mobile phone propose to his girlfriend? **He gave her a ring!**

• How do trees use a computer? **They log in!**

• Why did the computer go to the opticians? **It needed to improve its web-sight!**

DAD'S JOKES ABOUT NATURE

- Can a kangaroo jump higher than a house? **Of course they can, houses can't jump!**

- What do you call an alligator in a vest? **An investigator!**

- Why are pigs no good at team sports? **They always hog the ball!**

- Why do dogs float in water? **Because they're good buoys!**

- What do cows use to wash their hair? **Shamoo!**

- I just adopted a dog from a local blacksmith. **As soon as I got him home he made a bolt for the door!**

- What do you call an equine veterinary clinic? **A horse-pital.**

- Why don't they play poker in the jungle? **Too many cheetahs!**

- I took the shell off my racing snail, in the hope it would go faster. **But if anything, it just**

made it more sluggish!

- Where do animals go when their tails fall off? **The retail store!**

- How many tickles does it take to tickle an octopus? **Tentacles!**

- What do you call a bear without any teeth? **A gummy bear!**

- What days do fish dislike the most? **Fri-days!**

- My dog used to chase people on a scooter. **It got so bad I had**

to take his scooter away!

- What do cows do at the weekends? **They go to the Moooovies!**

- Spring is here! **I got so excited I wet my plants!**

- Is it true that humans eat more bananas than monkeys. **Of course it's true, I've never seen anyone eat a monkey!**

- What kind of car does a sheep like to drive? **A Lamborghini!**

- Why do ducks have tail feathers? **To cover up their butt quacks!**

- What do you call a sleeping dinosaur? **A tyrannosaurus rest!**

- If the earth was flat and fish swan over the edge, where would they go? **Trout-er space!**

- What do you call a fish that likes to play golf? **A golfish!**

- Why do you never see an elephant hiding in trees? **Because they're so good at it!**

- What did the Koala pack for his weekend away? **Just the bear essentials!**

- Why did the bird buy the nest? **Because it was cheep!**

- What's the scariest plant in the jungle? **Bam-BOO!**

- What do you call a dinosaur fart? **A blast from the past!**

- Why did the dog bark when it stepped on the sandpaper? **It was too ruff!**

- What do they call the Italian Bigfoot? **Spaghetti squach!**

- The best place to weigh whales is **at a whale weigh station.**

- Where's the best place to see whales? **Also at the whale weigh station!**

- Where's the best place to feed a whale? **No, silly, not at the whale weigh station, in the ocean where they live!**

- What do you call an elephant that doesn't matter? **An irrelephant!**

• What do you call a fly without wings? **A walk!**

• What did Dad say when the cat was sick on the mat. **'It's not feline well!'**

• Why do the seagulls fly over the ocean? **Because if they flew over the bay we would call them bagels!**

• I went into a pet shop. I said, 'I'd like to buy a goldfish.' The guy said, 'Do want an aquarium?' **I said, 'I'm not interested what star sign it is!'**

• Why was the bird sick? **It had the**

FLEW and its throat was SOAR!

· What do you call a bowtie wearing fish? **So-fish-ticated!**

· What do you get from pampered cows? **Spoiled milk!**

· What do you call a cow that plays a violin? **A mooosician!**

· Dad says they measure snakes in inches **as they don't have feet!**

· What do you call a pony with a sore throat? **A little hoarse!**

- I ordered a chicken and an egg online…. **I'll let you know!**

- What's the best selling insect? **A deodor-ant!**

- What do you call two monkeys that share an Amazon account? **Prime mates!**

- I just watched a documentary about beavers. **It was the best dam show I ever saw!**

- What's the loudest pet you can get? **A trumpet!**

- What kind of magic do cows believe in? **MooDoo!**

- My dog's clever, I asked him what's two minus two. **He said nothing!**

DAD'S MOVIES JOKES

- What do you call James Bond when he takes a bath? **Bubble 07**.

- What did Obi-wan say at the rodeo? **'Use the horse, Luke!'**

- Why was Spartacus not upset when the lion ate his wife? **Because he was Gladiator!**

- What's Dr. Fauci's favorite movie? **The Mask!**

• I was driving home when suddenly a group of robbers jumped in and stole everything. **They were pirates of the car I be in!**

• I started following Vin Diesel on Instagram. **He's a tough actor to follow!**

• I knew I had a drinking problem. Then one day I broke into a Hollywood movie set and spanked Dwayne Johnson right on the butt. **That's when I knew I'd hit Rock bottom!**

• A couple went to a marriage

counselor. 'I've had enough,' she said. 'With his Star Wars costumes, toys, and DVDs. All the constant references to the films, it's too much I'm leaving.' **'Hmmm,' commented her husband. 'Divorce is strong with this one!'**

- Be careful about trusting zombies. **I hear they are rotten people!**

- What do you call it when Tom Cruise drives your car? **Cruise control!**

- How do you know Will Smith's footprints in the snow? **They are the fresh-prints!**

- How do you make Lady Gaga cry? **Poker face!**

- How did Reese eat her ice cream? **Witherspoon!**

- On a scale of one to ten, how obsessed with Harry Potter are you? **About nine and three quarters!**

- What do you call a gunslinger with glasses? **Squint Eastwood!**

- Why did the angry Jedi cross the road? **To get to the dark side!**

• What do you call a Tom Cruise movie about cooking? **A Few Good Menus!**

• What kind of mail does a movie vampire get? **Fang mail.**

• Why did the vampire give up acting? **He couldn't find a part he could sink his teeth into!**

• What Jedi can you eat? **Obi Wan Cannoli!**

• What is the blue whale's favorite James Bond movie? **License to Krill.**

- What is a dentist's favorite movie? **Plaque to the Future!**

- What's a bee's favorite movie? **Beauty and the Bees!**

- What's a llama's favorite movie? **Llamadeus!**

- Have you seen the film called 'Farts?' **I wouldn't, it really stinks!**

- I just heard Back to the Future is getting a re-release at the movies. **It's about time!**

DAD'S HOSPITAL JOKES

• Yesterday Dad accidentally ate some food coloring. The doctor said he was okay **but Dad thought he'd dyed a little inside!**

• A hare, a bunny and a rabbi walk into a blood donation lab. **The rabbi says I'm probably a Type O.**

• Did you hear Captain Ahab was too sick to hunt Moby Dick. **I hope he gets whale soon!**

• The patient said, 'Can I

administer my own anesthetic?'
The surgeon replied, 'Go ahead, knock yourself out!'

- The patient says, I accidentally swallowed a bunch of scrabble tiles. **The doctor replies, that's serious, your next trip to the bathroom could spell DISASTER!**

- I had a neck brace fitted last year. **Since then I've never looked back!**

- Pupils are one of the last parts of the body to stop working after you die. **They dilate!**

• The World Health Organization has declared that dogs cannot transmit coronavirus, so there's no reason to quarantine them anymore. **W.H.O. let the dogs out!**

• What's the best time to go to the dentist? **Tooth-hurty!**

• Why do nurses like red crayons? **They sometimes have to draw blood!**

• Which wolf would you ask for directions? **A where-wolf!**

• What do you give a sick

lemon? **Lemon-aid!**

- My doctor told me I was going deaf. **That news was hard for me to hear!**

- Did you hear about the man who lost his left leg and arm in an accident? **He's all right now!**

- My nasal congestion is getter better. **'snot so bad today!**

- A young boy swallows some coins and is taken to the hospital. When his dad calls to ask how he is, he's told, **'No change yet!'**

• I tried playing hide and seek in the hospital, **but they kept finding me in the ICU.**

• A man goes to the hospital and says, 'Doctor, I think I'm a bit hard of hearing.' The doctor replies, 'Can you describe the symptoms?' **The man says, 'Sure, Marge has blue hair and Homer is fat and bald!'**

• Who is the coolest person in the hospital? **The Ultra Sound guy!**

• Who stands in for him on his day's off? **The Hip replacement guy!**

• A guy goes to the doctor, 'It hurts when I touch my neck, my arm or my chest.' **The doctor replies, 'You've broken your finger!'**

• A man goes to the doctor and says, 'I keep seeing a werewolf with big sharp teeth!' The doctor asks, 'Have you seen a psychiatrist?' **The man replies, 'No, just the werewolf.'**

• What did the doctor tell the patient who said he thought his eyes were changing color? **'It's just a pigment of your imagination!'**

• Had to wait ages for my Xray today. **There was only a skeleton staff working!**

• Did you hear about the dermatologist **who started his career from scratch?**

• I was asked to leave the hospital after saying to a Covid 19 patient, **'Stay positive!'**

• Why did the hospital send their nurses to art school? **To learn how to draw blood!**

• Doctor: 'We've admitted your wife to hospital.' Me: 'How is she?'

Doctor: 'I'm afraid she's critical.'
Me: 'You get used to that!'

• 'I think I'm a moth,' the man told the doctor. 'You probably want to see a psychiatrist for that,' was the reply. 'Yes, I know,' answered the man. 'Then why are you here?' asked the confused doctor. **The man replied, 'The light was on!'**

• A man who thinks he is a piece of luggage has been admitted to a hospital. **Psychiatrists say he's the strangest case they've ever come across!**

• I went to a urologist who told

me I needed a cystoscopy. I asked him what's that? **He said, 'we're going to Youtube your Peetube!'**

• What's the most common operation in a LEGO hospital? **Plastic surgery, of course!**

• Patient: 'Doctor, I think I swallowed a pillow.' Doctor: 'How do you feel?' **Patient: 'A little down in the mouth!'**

DAD WORK JOKES

• Dad didn't land the job at the Amazon depot. **Surprising, as we all thought he was a prime candidate!**

• I just started a business where we specialize in weighing tiny objects. **It's a small-scale operation!**

• Dad gave up his job repairing crystal balls. **He couldn't see a future in it.**

• Dad was fired from his job for making too many egg-jokes. **He was laid off!**

- I was fired from my job at the bed store. **Who duvet think they are?**

- Did you hear about the butcher who backed into his meat grinder? **He got a little behind in his work!**

- Dad quit his job at the Helium factory. **Said he won't be spoken to in that tone!**

- I was fired from a canned juice company. **Apparently I couldn't concentrate!**

- I didn't want to believe Dad was stealing from his job as a road worker. **But when I got home all the signs were there!**

- I've got a great joke about construction, **but I'm still working on it!**

- I used to work in a shoe shop... **it didn't pay much but it was good for the sole!**

- My boss said to me, 'this is the fifth time you've come into work late this week. Do you know what this means?' **'Yes,' I replied, 'it's Friday!'**

· Did you hear about the man who fell into the upholstery machine? **Good news, he's fully recovered!**

· I used to have a job at a calendar factory, **but got the sack when I took a couple of days off!**

· My wife left me because of all the overtime I'm doing as a security guard at the airport. As she walked out I said, **'Did you pack your own bags?'**

· My boss told me to have a good day. **So I went home!**

- They ran out of product at the ironworks. To keep running they had to beg, borrow, and steel!

- Why did dad get fired from the banana factory? **He kept throwing away the bent ones!**

- The first five days after the weekend **are the hardest!**

- Why did the can crusher quit his job? **Because it was soda depressing!**

- I got a job at a paperless office. **Everything was great until I**

needed to use the bathroom!

• My memory has gotten so bad it has caused me to lose my job. **I'm still employed, I just can't remember where!**

• My employment application asked who is to be notified in case of emergency. **I wrote, 'A very good doctor!'**

• A committee is twelve people **doing the work of one!**

• My annual performance review says I lack 'passion and intensity.'

I guess management hasn't seen me alone with a Big Mac!

• Here's some advice, at a job interview tel them you are willing to give 110 percent. **Unless, of course, you're applying to be a statistician!**

• I went for an interview for an office job today. The interviewer told me I'd start at \$2,000 a month then after 6 months I'll be on \$2,500 a month. **I told them I'll start in a month!**

• I was really upset at work today. The computers went down so we had to do everything manually, **it took 20 minutes to**

shuffle the cards for Solitaire!

• Dad quit his job at the donut factory. **Said he was fed up with the hole business!**

DAD'S JOKES ABOUT EVERYTHING

- What did the pen say to the rock? **Nothing, because pens can't talk!**

- What do you call a can opener that doesn't work? **A can't opener!**

- Why do truckers like October 4th the best? **Because it's 10-4, good buddy!**

- My grandfather brought down 6 German planes in WW2. **Worst mechanic the Luftwaffe ever had.**

• Why did the lawyer show up in court in his underwear? **He forgot his lawsuit!**

• How do you throw a party in outer space? **You planet!**

• Ghosts are bad liars because **you can see right through them!**

• Why can't a bike stand on its own? **Because it's two tired!**

• I hate it when people say age is only a number. **Age is clearly a word!**

- I'm reading a horror story in Braille. **Something bad is going to happen, I can just feel it!**

- Dropped a six pack of beer on my foot. **No serious injury, just a small brews!**

- They say there are plenty of fish in the sea **but all I want is a classic story of gull meets bouy!**

- If a child refuses to nap, **are they guilty of resisting a rest?**

- Does anyone need an

ark? **I Noah guy!**

- When I was young people used to cover me in chocolate and cream, and put a cherry on my head. **Life was tough in the gateau!**

- What do you call a fat psychic? **A four-chin teller!**

- The man who invented auto-correct has died. **His funfair is on sundial at moon.**

- It's hard to explain puns to kleptomaniacs… **they always take things literally!**

- What do stormy clouds wear? **Thunderwear!**

- What is the scariest city in the US? **Eerie, PA!**

- I've been struggling to become a good mountain climber. **It's an uphill battle!**

- What key do you use to open a banana? **A mon-key!**

- What kind of music did the pilgrims listen to? **Plymouth Rock!**

- I just did my laundry and now I'm super nervous. **There's a lot on the line!**

- I went to the bank this morning and they said I would need to verify my identity. **So I looked in a mirror and said, 'yep, that's me!'**

- What country's capital is growing the fastest? Ireland. **Every day it's Dublin!**

- A truck load of Brillo pads were stolen in a raid. **The police are scouring the area!**

- The man who invented speedboats has unfortunately passed away. **His funeral is on Friday, 10am followed by a wake!**

- Don't trust trees, says dad, **they seem kinda shady!**

- 'I'm afraid for the calendar,' said Dad. **'It's days are numbered!'**

- I was limbo dancing when a pickpocket stole my wallet. **How can anyone stoop so low!**

- Why are fart jokes so funny?

They buttcrack you up!

- Ever since I bought that little figurine the kids won't go into the back yard. **It's a gnome man's land now!**

- What musical instrument do you find in a bathroom? **A tuba toothpaste!**

- What has four wheels and flies? **A garbage truck!**

- What's made out of brass and sounds like Tom Jones? **Trombones!**

• I didn't really enjoy my posh childhood. Everything was handed to me on a plate. **Soup was a nightmare!**

• I used to play piano by ear. **Now I use my hands!**

• Just called the airline and asked the flight time between London and New York? She said, "just a minute...". **"Wow," I replied, "that's impressive."**

• I thought out of all these puns at least one in 10 would make me laugh. **But no pun in 10 did!**

- And a big shout out to my fingers. **I can count on all of them!**

- Why are Saturday and Sunday the strongest days? **Because the rest are weekdays!**

- Two guys walk into a bar. **Which is pretty stupid cause after the first guy walked into it you think the second guy would have seen it!**

- Another two guys walk into a bar. **The third guy ducked!**

- A guy walks into a bar. **And was**

disqualified from the limbo contest!

• A sandwich walks into a bar. **The barman says, "Sorry, we don't serve food here!"**

• Bono and The Edge walk into a bar. **The barman looks at them and says, 'Oh no, not U2 again!'**

• 'Hey, Bartender, a word of advice. Don't push Bono, **he's close to the Edge!'**

• Remembering all the people who said I was too lazy to achieve anything in life, **is what gets me**

out of bed in the afternoon!

• The first time I saw a universal remote control I thought to myself, **'well, this changes everything!'**

• I wrote a pop tune about a tortilla, **but it's more of a wrap song!**

• Why are elevator jokes so good? **They work on many levels!**

• What's orange and sounds like a parrot? **A carrot!**

• Mr. Turner; Mr Cruz; Mr

Danson. **Thank you for coming to my Ted Talk!**

• What do you get when you cross a snowman with a vampire? **Frostbite!**

• Why is no-one friends with vampires? **They're a pain in the neck!**

• How do vampires show they are sick? **They're coffin!**

• What's it like to be kissed by a vampire? **It's a pain in the neck!**

- Where do vampires keep their money? **In a blood bank!**

- Where do polar bears keep their money? **In a snow bank!**

- A man dies after falling into a giant coffee vat. **The police report he didn't suffer, it was instant!**

- I ate a clock the other day. **It was very time consuming!**

- Never argue with an idiot - **they drag you down to their level then beat you with experience!**

- Is this pool safe for diving? **It deep-ends.**

- Which can you do faster. A half Windsor, a full Windsor, or a standard Bow. **In the end it's a tie!**

- What do you call a belt of watches? **A waist of time!**

- I could go on and on about the virtues of underwear. **But I'll be brief!**

- How do you talk to a giant? **You use big words!**

- Did you hear the joke about the blunt pencil? **Wasn't worth it, it was pointless!**

- Dad said whenever mom is sad he lets her draw things on him. **He gives her a shoulder to crayon!**

- Why did the man fall down the well? **Because he didn't see that well!**

- When do skeletons laugh? **When something tickles their funny bone!**

- Why is Peter Pan always flying? **It's obvious, he Neverlands!**

- WARNING - Dirty Joke. How can you tell when a plant is scared? **It soils itself!**

- I don't play soccer because I enjoy the sport. **I do it for the kicks!**

- Common sense is like a deodorant. **Those who need it the most never seem to use it!**

- Rest in peace boiling water. **You will be mist!**

- Where do boats go when they are sick? **To the boat-doc!**

- How do you make Holy Water? **You boil the hell out of it!**

- Want to hear a joke about paper? **Never mind, it's tearable!**

- What do you call a boomerang that doesn't come back? **A stick!**

- What did Tennessee? **The same thing as Arkansas!**

- I heard there is a new shop called Moderation. **It has everything!**

- My neighbor tiled my roof for free. **He said it was on the house!**

- Why did the coach yell at the vending machine? **He wanted his quarter-back!**

- 2017 didn't jog: Also didn't jog during 2018, nor 2019, nor 2020, and guess what, didn't jog in 2021: **This is a running joke!**

- Where do crayons go on vacation? **Color-ado!**

- My weighing machine was stolen

from my bathroom. **I'm launching a full-scale investigation!**

- I want to show you my clock collection. **But that would take up too much time!**

- I'm going to sell my vacuum cleaner - **it's just gathering dust!**

- What did the mountain climber name his son? **Cliff!**

- Somebody is sending me flowers with the heads cut off. **I think I'm being stalked.**

- I laid in my sleeping bag, staring up at the stars. **And thought, who stole my tent?!**

- The odd thing about parenting is that by the time you are experienced at the job, **you're then unemployed!**

- Why don't skeletons go trick or treating? **It really is sad, cause they have no-body to go with!**

- What does a sprinter eat before a race? **Nothing, they fast!**

- Where do wasps like to have

lunch? **A Bee-stro!**

- I slept like a log last night. **I woke up in the fireplace!**

- How funny are mountains? **They're hill-areas!**

- What has more letters than the alphabet? **The post office!**

- Did you hear about the hungry clock? **It went back for seconds!**

- This man calls 911 in a panic, 'My wife is having a baby. The

contractions are coming really fast!'
"Calm down," says the operator. 'Is
this her first child?' **'No," shouts
the guy, "this is her husband!'**

• Why did the mobile phone go for an
eye test? **Because it lost its contacts!**

• Two cannibals were eating a
clown. **One says to the other,
'does this taste funny to you?'**

• Want to hear a time travel joke?
Never mind, you already heard it!

• Singing in the shower is fun
till you get soap in your mouth.

Then it's a soap opera!

• What do a tick and the Eiffel Tower have in common? **They are both Paris-sites!**

• Why was the golfer crying? **He was going through a rough patch!**

• Why can't you hear a psychiatrist using the bathroom? **Because the P is silent!**

• England doesn't have a kidney bank. **But it does have a Liverpool!**

- And did you hear about the giant who threw up? **It's all over town!**

- If April showers bring May flowers, what do May flowers bring? **Pilgrims!**

- Did you hear the rumor about butter? **I'd better not tell you, I don't want to spread it around!**

- Nostalgia **isn't what it used to be!**

- I don't trust stairs. **They're always up to something!**

· What did the ocean say to the beach? **Nothing, it just waved!**

· What do you call a factory that makes okay products? **A satisfactory!**

· What's made of leather and sounds like a sneeze? **A shoe!**

· I wasn't going to get a brain transplant. **But I changed my mind!**

· Two hats were hanging on a rack. One said, '**You stay here, I'll go on a head!**'

- Did you hear about the brewery night watchman who fell into a vat of beer and drowned? It was a long lingering death. **It would have been quicker but he got out three times to go pee.**

- Did you hear about the man who fell into a lens grinding machine? **He made a spectacle of himself!**

- How come was your hair cut so quickly? **Because the barber knew a short-cut!**

- I was wondering why the frisbee kept looking bigger and

bigger. **Then it hit me!**

• What did the janitor say when he jumped out of the closet? **Supplies!**

• I used to be addicted to the Hokey Cokey, **but I managed to turn myself around!**

• A man heard that most accidents happen within two miles of home. **So he moved!**

• Did you hear about the new chocolate record player? **It sounds pretty sweet!**

- A two seater Cessna plane crashed into a cemetery. **So far 516 bodies have been recovered.**

- The little boy said to his dad, "I only know 25 letters of the alphabet. **I don't know Y."**

- How does the moon cut his hair? **Eclipse it!**

- What did one wall say to the other? **I'll meet you at the corner!**

- I wouldn't buy anything with velcro. **It's a rip off!**

• People are making apocalypse jokes **like there's no tomorrow!**

• What did the skeleton say to the bartender? **"I'll have a beer and a mop!"**

• A blue and red ship crashed in the Pacific. **Apparently the survivors have been marooned!**

• Did you hear the story about the haunted elevator? **It raised my spirits!**

• A cop caught two kids with a

firework and a battery. **He charged one and let the other off!**

- When in France where do fruits go on vacation? **Pear-is!**

- What did Baby Corn say to Mama Corn? **Where's Pop Corn?**

- What did Beethoven become after he died? **A decomposer!**

- I dreamt I was drowning in a ocean of orange soda. **Then I realized it was just a Fanta Sea!**

- What's the advantage of living in Switzerland? **Well, the flag is a big plus!**

- My sister thinks I don't give her enough privacy. **At least that's what she said in her dairy.**

- There's a new type of broom that is selling well. **It's sweeping the nation!**

- What did the pirate say on his 80th birthday? **"Aye Matey!"**

- Does anyone know how to charge milk? **Because mine is stuck at 2%!**

- What did the fish say when he swan into a wall? **Damn!**

- Why do scuba divers fall backwards into the water? **Because if they fell forward they'd still be in the boat!**

- Why are piggy banks so wise? **They are full of common cents!**

- Three things happen when you get to my age, said Dad. **'First you start to lose your memory and I've forgotten the other two!'**

- Dad says that maybe he's getting

older but he's still got it. **Mom says, 'The trouble is nobody wants it!'**

- Mom says 'Dad is so old that a fireman has to be in attendance **every time he lights his birthday candles!'**

- Mom says dad is so old **he has Jesus' beeper number!**

- Mom says Dad is so old at his party **his candles cost more than the birthday cake!**

- Mom says dad is so old **his back goes out more than he does!**

- Mom says Dad is so old **he and his teeth don't sleep together!**

- What do you call a snobbish criminal coming down the stairs? **A con-descending!**

- Why didn't the skeleton cross the road? **Because he didn't have any guts!**

- How does a one armed man tie his shoe laces? **Single handedly!**

- Did you know that diarrhea is hereditary. **It runs in your jeans.**

- What did one tomato say to the other. **I know I'm late but I'll ketchup!**

- Why was the archaeologist upset? **His job was in ruins!**

- How do you cut an ocean in half? **With a sea-saw.**

- Milk is the fastest liquid in the world. **It's pasteurized before you even see it!**

- What award did the knock knock joke writer win? **The no-bell prize!**

- Dad asked mom, do you think I'm vain? She said, no, why do you ask? He said, **guys as good-looking as me usually are!**

- What sits on the bottom of the sea and twitches? **A nervous wreck!**

- What lays on the ocean and shouts rude words at passing boats? **Crude oil!**

- What do you call a person with no body and no nose? **Nobody knows!**

- Why can't a hand be 12 inches long?

Because then it would be a foot!

- The invisible man married the invisible woman. **The kids were nothing to look at!**

- Two TV antennas got married, the wedding wasn't much **but the reception was excellent!**

- What did the 0 say to the 8? **Nice belt!**

- Where did Napoleon keep his armies? **Up his sleevies!**

- Would glass coffins sell well? **Remains to be seen!**

- What's the difference between a hobo on a trike and a gentleman on a bike? **Attire!**

- What did the policeman say to his belly button? **You're under a vest!**

- Last night your dad and I watched two DVDs back to back. **Luckily I was the one facing the TV!**

- How do you get a farm girl's attention? **A-tractor!**

• Did you hear about the cartoonist found dead at his home? **Details are sketchy!**

• Why did the scarecrow win employee of the month? **Because he was outstanding in his field!**

• I asked my son when he got the chocolate he was eating even though the shops were closed. **He said he still had a few Twix up his sleeve.**

• Do they have loud laughing in Hawaii? **No, just a low ha!**

- Do you know why eggs don't tell each other jokes? **They'd crack each other up!**

- Why didn't the bicycle stand up by itself? **It was two tired!**

- The man who created the shovel **made a groundbreaking invention.**

- What's the best way to cut down a tree? **Depends who's axing!**

- Give me an example of chocolate pronouns. **Her/she!**

- I used to have an addition to soap. **But I'm clean now!**

- What does a lemon say when it's answering the phone? **Yellow!**

- What time did dad go to the dentist? **Tooth-hurt-y!**

- Why are graveyards crowded? **People are dying to get in!**

- What kind of car does an egg drive? **A Yolkswagon!**

· I burned 2000 calories today. **I left my food in the oven too long!**

· What's the longest word in the English language? Smiles. **The first and last letter are a mile apart!**

· Dad said he would buy me a telescope since I was so interested in astronomy. **I said I'd look into it!**

· What kind of prize do you give somebody who hasn't moved a muscle in a year? **A-trophy!**

· It was so cold the other day

I saw a street-thief with his hands in his own pockets!

- I was going to tell you about my car's broken horn. **But it doesn't sound right!**

- I was just reminiscing about the beautiful herb garden I had when growing up. **Good thymes!**

- How does a taco say grace? **Lettuce pray!**

- Mom asked dad to put the cat out. **He said he didn't know it was on fire!**

- What's it called when a snowman throws a tantrum? **A meltdown!**

- What does a bee use to brush its hair? **A honeycomb!**

- How do you make a tissue dance? **Put a little boogie in it!**

- Why did the orange lose the race? **It ran out of juice!**

- How do you fix a broken pumpkin? **With a pumpkin patch!**

- Why are fish so smart? **They live in schools!**

- What did the sink tell the toilet? **You look flushed!**

- What has ears but cannot hear? **A cornfield!**

- I was really angry at my friend Mark for stealing my dictionary. **I told him, 'Mark, my words!'**

- What food is best at board games? **Chess nuts!**

- Why are skeletons so calm? **Because nothing gets under their skin!**

- What did the father buffalo say to his kid when he dropped him off at school? **Bi-son!**

- What social network does your grandmother use? **Instagranny!**

- What's brown and sticky? **A stick, of course!**

- Why didn't the watermelons run away and get married.

Because they cantaloupe!

- Did you hear about the joke about the roof? **Never mind, it's over your head!**

- How do you deal with a fear of speed bumps? **You slowly get over it!**

- What do houses wear? **An address!**

- What do you call a sleeping bull? **A bulldozer!**

- How does a lawyer say good bye? **I'll be suing ya!**

- How does a ghost stay safe in a car? **He puts on his sheet belt!**

- What's smarter than a wasp that knows the alphabet? **A spelling bee!**

- What do you call ten guys waiting for a haircut? **A barberqueue!**

- When two vegans get into an argument **is it still called a beef?**

- A cheese factory exploded in France. **Da Brie was everywhere!**

- What happens when you boil a funny bone? **It becomes laughing stock!**

- Why did the fireman retire? **He was burned out!**

- What runs but can't walk? **A faucet!**

- I have a fear of lifts. **But I'm taking steps to cure it!**

- What kind of shoes do Ninjas wear? **Sneakers!**

- How does a penguin build its house? **Igloos it together!**

- I used to be addicted to soap, **but I'm clean now!**

- Why do seafood restaurant chefs always end up single? **Because they are shellfish lovers!**

- What did two pieces of bread say when they dated? **It was loaf at first sight!**

- Why do pancakes always win at baseball? **They have the best batter!**

- Why were sirens blaring when the ocean was starting to form? **Because it was an emergent sea!**

- What kind of horses come out after the sun sets? **Nightmares!**

- I'd look good with a bow made of wood around my neck. **Wooden tie?**

- What do you call a cheese that's not yours? **Nacho cheese!**

- Dad went to the bookstore and saw a book called, 'How to Solve 50% of Your Problems'.

He bought two of them!

- What do you say to a rabbit on its birthday? **Hoppy Birthday!**

- My boss asked me to restock the herbs before I left. **I said I couldn't as I was out of thyme!**

- Why did the envelope take so long to get ready? **It had to get addressed!**

- How do you throw a party in space? **You planet!**

- What type of tree fits in

your hand? **A palm tree!**

- Why was the broom late for class? **It overslept!**

- What do you call a pencil with two erasers? **Pointless!**

- Can February March? **No, but April May!**

- That car looks good **but the muffler looks ex-hausted!**

- And now..... drum roll please, the last Dad Joke in the book!